I APOLOGIZE IN ADVANCE FOR THE AWFUL THINGS I'M GONNA DO

This publication (c)2014 by Danny Bland & Greg Dulli

Distributed by Sub Pop

2013 Fourth Avenue
Third Floor
Seattle, WA 98121 USA
www.subpop.com

FOREWORD

Danny Bland is a man of few words and even fewer syllables. Over
the years, as my road manager/co-conspirator, he and I have driven
300 or 400 miles in a day, from one show to another, and sometimes
the only conversation we'll have will be "Do you feel like eating
a burger or Mexican food?" or "I used to know a wild girl in that
town. I wonder what the hell ever happened to her." We save the
deeper stuff for the stage or the songs or the poetry. Because of
this, I have no idea where or how Danny discovered the traditional
Japanese poetic form of haiku. I have no idea why the haiku, trea-
sured and used by many poets from Auden to Cummings to Ginsberg to
Collins, appealed to him but I can guess. The haiku's simple complex-
ity of 5 syllables - 7 syllables - 5 syllables, suits his personality
perfectly: direct, vivid, tough, and honest.

   Narrow Roads to the Interior is the title of a collection of poems
by the beloved 17th Century Japanese haiku master, Basho. Like the
itinerant Basho, Danny is a wandering poet who has truly traveled on
some narrow roads as well as broad, endless interstate highways and
maddening, deadening airports. His travels have taken him from the
heat-soaked, desert streets of Phoenix to Istanbul's ancient Hagia
Sophia, from the Kamchatka Peninsula's desolate forests to the hope-
less, heroin-soaked back alleys of Seattle. More importantly, like
all good poets, Danny has also traveled to "the interior" of his
heart and soul. His deeply personal haikus are funny, serious, pain-
ful, and fearless. At times shocking, then abruptly, surprisingly
tender, his poems constantly question accepted beliefs and attitudes,
both society's and his own. Like the classic blues singers, Danny
is able to use a limited form to express the limitless. Not a simple
task by any means. He is one hell of a writer and companion. One of
these days, on one of those 400-mile drives, I'll have to discuss
all this poetry jazz with Danny. Or, maybe, we'll just discuss what
burger joint to eat at next.

                                                      — DAVE ALVIN

                              • • •

Greg Dulli's photographs take you places. Places where dark and
murky and mirth and joyous co-mingle, perhaps even slow dance.
Places that appeal to your inner scoundrel, your ne'er-do-well, the
bad neighborhood in your mind. A place where photography is more
about eye and opportunity and storytelling than it is about equip-
ment. A place where you can finally be comfortable admitting you're
not a voyeur but a low down dirty peeper. Or maybe that's just me.

                                                      — DANNY BLAND

FOR ISABEL, MARY JANE AND SAM

you open your arms
still undaunted by the threat
of being eaten

in polite whispers
my behavior has been coined
"at best, unseemly"

when the day is done
you light a cigarette, pick
spiders from my hair

I'm not well, I pray
and lift the virgin mary's
skirt at the same time

find your place in my
ribcage, sleep soundly knowing
your secrets are safe

SHE POPPED HER GUM. "LET'S
DO BAD THINGS IN THE FUNHOUSE."
MOM WAITS IN THE CAR

baby, quit making
me smile. it creeps people out
when I do that shit

I saw the devil
in jackson square, she was six,
apocalyptic

caffeine, nicotine,
fear not the other drugs; you're
my heart's desire

next waiter who asks
if I'm your father will get
a fork in the throat

leopard print converse
on the dash, straw to your lips
a perfect moment

they meet at sternum
barely hid in paper skin
hardly safe from me

when I hear average
people's "wild stories," I
am the devil, mute

she holds a piece of
duct tape to her lips, breathes in
a boy she once knew

she covered the walls
with visqueen, sat one last time
at her vanity

sometimes I miss the
days of wine and roses, I
mean, dope and bushmills

horror movies are
like women; when they're bad, I
like them even more

note at the front desk:
wish I'd cut your tongue out and
taken it with me

she will sit upon
a throne made of human skulls
and smile so sweetly

ATTEMPTING FIRST BASE,
DRIVE-IN MOVIE PROJECTOR,
HER STELLAR DEFENSE

FIRST in the MORNiNG
FUCKiNG YOU is ALL i WANT
THAT, THEN SOME COFFEE

seen bloody handprints
in fifty dollar rooms, seen
beautiful things too

"son, girls that smoke and
have tattoos are just dirty,
find one right away"

the square, the table
the place we have agreed to
meet as battered ghosts

your self-inflicted
wounds taste of salt, somehow paint
a pretty picture

some like blondes, some like
brunettes. I like a girl who
gives good blasphemy

say motherfucker
as often as possible
waitresses love it

turn ons: wise-cracking
malcontents with lax morals,
turn offs: sunshine, cats

forgive my mother
she is Dr. Frankenstein
in theory only

the sign blinks "live girls,"
and it draws flies to honey,
empty your wallets

the dead pull my sleeve,
rest their heads on my shoulder,
someone to talk to

from across the room
I stared at you for twenty
years, waiting my turn

torches and pitchforks
outside my window tonight
the villagers know

THIS SH

ASS STUFF

PACK it FULL

MAY BE SHARP

THIS LIFE

SO I'M GONNA OF CRAZY

watched you as a child
pull hearts out of old men's chests
eat them like candy

something or someone
whispers nothings in your head
sweet or not, you hear

your fresh-fucked hair combed,
turtleneck covered bite marks
you look good as new

distance is madding
close-up works best in knife fights
and cupid's sweet hold

I'll blow the dust off.
you're dead to the rest of the
world, but not to me

I'll never leave you
without a tale to tell, a
scar, reason to smile

YOU'RE LICKING YOUR WOUNDS
ACROSS FROM THE BUS STATION
THE HOTEL CONGRESS

bible in the drawer
you mock old testament in
your sweet honey purr

there are days when I
need to spit on syllables
just to squeeze them in

nose to nose, growling
violent kiss untethered
dentist on speed-dial

we sat in silence
content to read minds, I watched
smoke dance from your lips

of all the daisies
she had to murder, only
one said "he loves me"

the devil is here
in the morning we will all
wake up with black eyes

YOU, A DROP
WAITING
TO OPEN

of SWEAT FELL,
FOR PERMISSION,
YOUR EYES

oh, poison ivy
are you stomping on pedals
or young monster hearts?

wrapped up in plastic,
buried in the woods, stapled
pages, so adored.

she had the dead-eyed
stare, the brass pole expertise
what she lacked was "it"

if you raise your hand
to my sisters, you will feel
the weight of us all

burn down your office
and smash your phone, let's just live
off of pockets picked

I bought a whiskey
for sister helen, discussed
saints, the football kind.

she remembered when
she was wild, dirty and free.
smiled, waved at her kids

in hotel lobbies
I hear laughter, see phantom
violin cases

if you're not ashamed
of some things you've done, I can
fix that. come over.

seems I got more sleep
when all I had to do was
chase girls and rob graves

leave your incisors
and a dirty black t-shirt,
so I won't miss you

coincidentally,
your ghosts crave spirits, something
to burn down their throats

you love your bruises,
your scars, your souvenirs of
reckless abandon

....

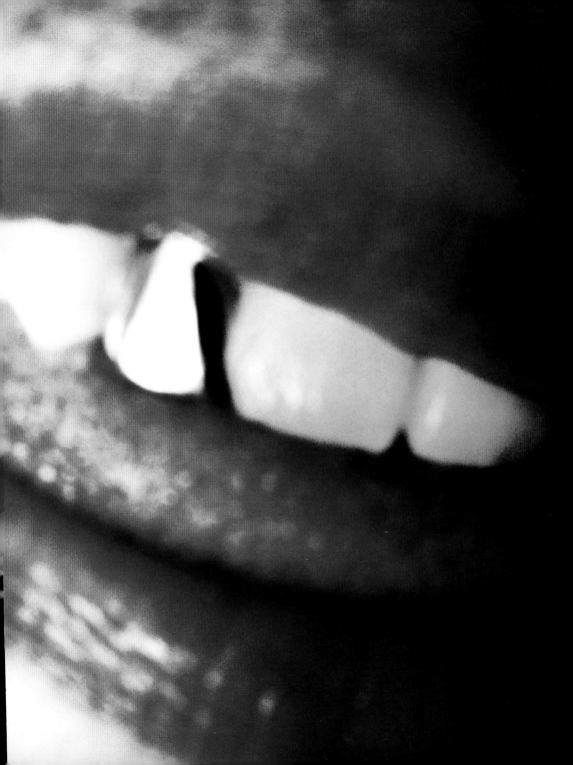

on her business card:
hip-shaker, god-denier,
knife enthusiast.

every morning, I
kiss each scar on your body
one through seventeen

trust me, I'll take it
with sweet words, bewitchment or
scalpel if needed.

some honeyed, dulcet.
some are not even poems,
just bumper stickers

no savagery, teeth,
serpent's tongue. it was a kiss
with nothing to prove

EXHALING THE SMOKE
THE FIREFLY DISTRACTS ME
FROM MY FILTHY PROSE

SURE, SHE BROKE A NAIL
AND HER KNUCKLES BLED, BUT NOT
AS MUCH AS HIS NOSE

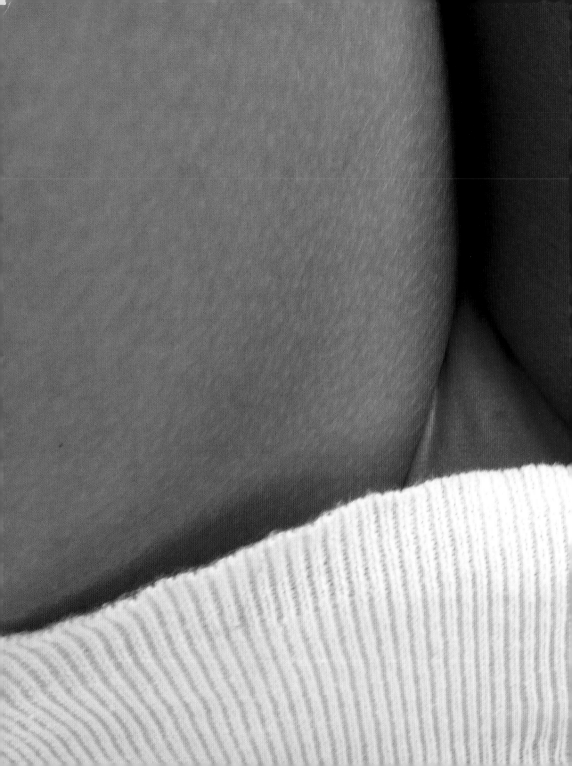

I say tomato
you say untreated, out of
control sex addict

she writes suicide
notes on napkins, leaves them as
tips for waitresses

don't be sad, darlin'
death is just another chance
to find each other

the answer will be
the same 'til you chew off my
last middle finger

the devil's reading
taking her red sharpie to
a romance novel

call me old-fashioned
but I'm still a big fan of
original sin

alarms disabled
someday, dear, I'll turn these days
upside-down for you

no one has a soul
don't worry big-legged women
Robert Plant's a fool

wrapped in polka dots
her hips can shake the dust off
scratchy old records

the note read: wearing
your hoodie, it smells like you,
not giving it back

she wants a story
no death, drugs or hospitals
got a dress instead

I fucking refuse
to go to the goddamn beach
fuck no, never

I like the slow burn
the love song I'll never write
the sweat-soaked shirt

as a child she played
psych ward scrabble, adding up
mother's made up words

on the hardwood floor
he whispers incantations
softly to her hips

unmanageable,
she poured a shot of whiskey,
stared at it awhile

I apologize
in advance for the awful
things I'm gonna do

drop my coins and bask
in all your pigtailed glory
soles stuck to the floor

he found a napkin
"don't destroy yourself for me"
written in lipstick

bed covered in ash
spilt wine, lipsticked paper cups
twenty for the maid

don't talk to strangers
or silky-coated chess cheats,
sweet margarita

the sun is rising
or perhaps, my love, the east
is bleeding slowly

once upon a time
he was devilish, if not
the devil himself

she smelled like red wine
and smiled the way she did
before she wrecked you

cherry-flavored mouth
the straw extracting bourbon
cigarette chaser

blinking motel lights
slash through the blinds, cut ribbons
across your torso

brand new, plasticky
hearts are dull, I prefer them
used and tossed aside

I say stigmata
and you say stigmato, let's
call the whole thing off

resuscitation
called for an ice cube in an
unfortunate place

to devour, or
perhaps, to fuck the goddamn
demons out of you

he was instructed,
place roses on the altar
to feel loved again

she placed the barrel
under her chin and smiled big
quick, take a picture

Huey P. Newton
refrigerator magnets
two for five dollars

SHE ATE CATFISH IN
HER SUNDAY CROWN OF GLORY
DEFINED TRUE BEAUTY

THE POCKET KNIFE CUT
HER   INITIALS IN HIS ARMS
IT WAS THEIR FIRST DATE

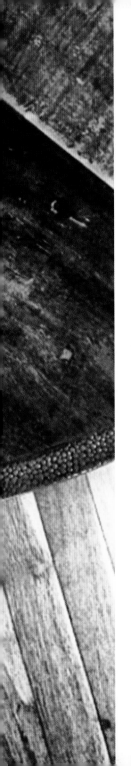

everybody knows
sideways for attention and
long way for results

· ·

a vacant pillow,
handwritten note. "love the way
you mess up my hair."

your beauty crawls in
and out of shadows, sometimes
coming up for air

are those lucky stars
southern hospitality
or just razor wire?

grandpa says he fucked
sophia loren on mars
and we believe him

don't you dare, she said
I'll crush your heart on the floor
like a cigarette

say what you will, I
still believe motherfucker
is the best cuss word

you'll cradle my skull
in your hands someday and laugh
just like I promised

the plunging neckline
amber shot glasses tilt back
a night to forget

I quit shooting dope,
drinking, stealing but I still
can't behave myself

seek impurity
with ruthless focus, my dear
bring it home to me

songs sneak up on you
some will slit your throat open
others stitch you up

spring is in the air
and a young man's fancy turns
to thoughts of relapse

you're wolvish, bloody
and ravenous. dirty talk
I learned from Shakespeare

• •

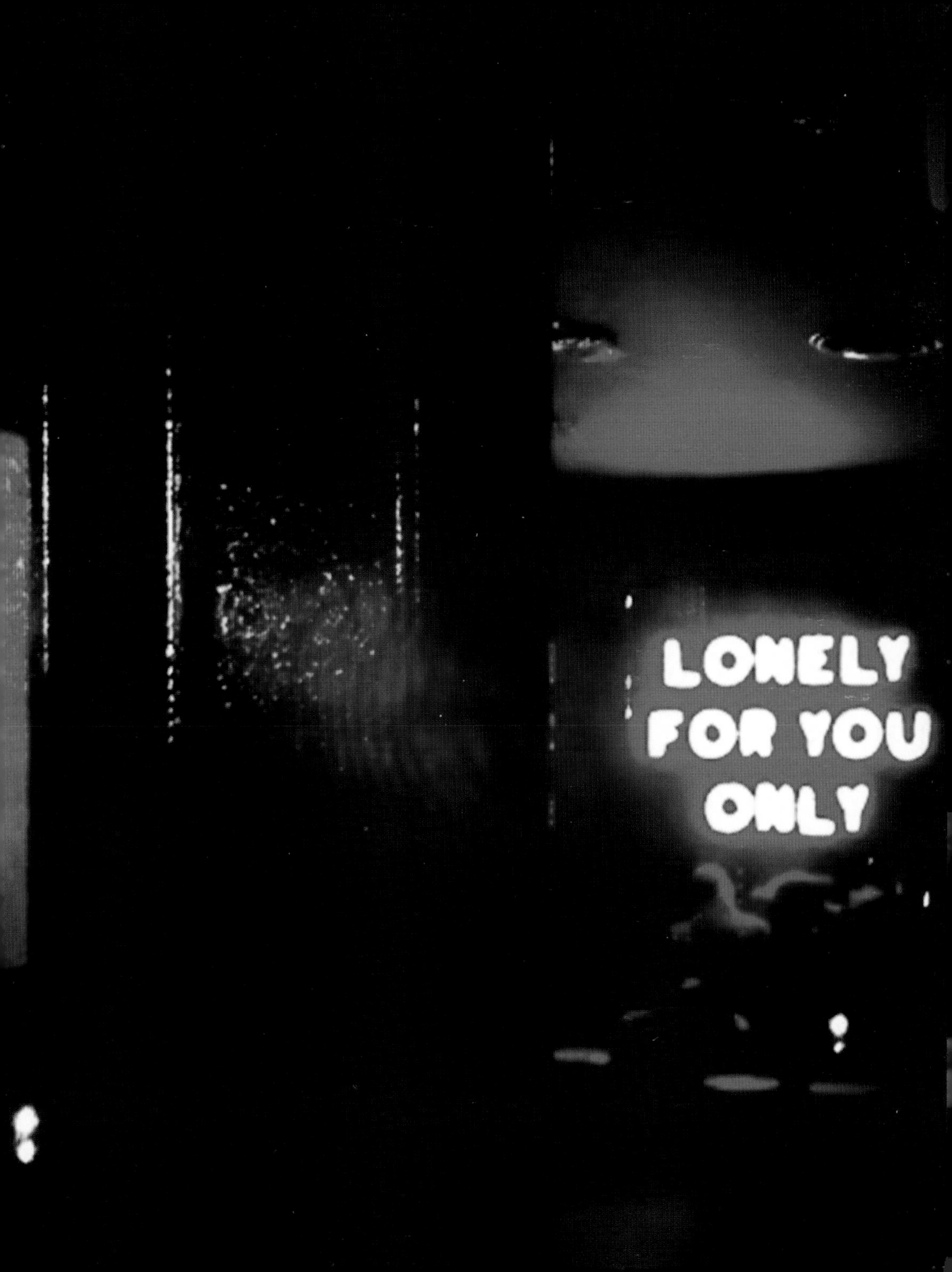
LONELY
FOR YOU
ONLY

SHE OLD MAN M
SoRts Thr
iN A LAUNL

tching HER
DIRTY PANTIES
RoNAL

in the melee of
blackout-curtained misconduct
you belong to me

took out her stitches
with a steak knife at shoney's
pretty as can be

his lips were sweet, the
stories they told enchanting
the lies; exhausting

filled the tub with bleach
and I lit the curtains on
fire, just in case

drawn and quartered, left
for dead, he still makes tea for
smoldering children

I have a thing for
ghosts who hold resined bows for
all eternity

•••

I hear confessions
nightly. you spill shameful tales
knowing I've done worse

the women I've known
have all been too good for me.
kind creatures, indeed

I hid the razors
you bought, you sucked the pills from
my throat, quid pro quo

she's a doll you found
in the attic; a doe-eyed,
sweet nest of spiders

our correspondence
sounds more violent threaty
than sweet love note-ish

bring champagne, you witch
throw a corpse on the fire, let's
get necromantic

I curse and you pray
but the oh my gods are not
intended for him

when the police came in
you were naked, cigarette
dangling from your lips

the belle of the ball
and the smut-selling pumpkin
drinking at midnight

in knowing glances,
your heart; full of fireworks
mine, wrought with spiders

the devil you know
kissed you through a chain link fence
tasting of sulfur

our bed, bedazzled
with cigarette burns at the
thunderbird motel

the imperfections
are where your real beauty lays
your scars are gorgeous

BE SAFE. I PLAN ON DOING HORRIBLE THINGS TO YOU IN THE FUTURE

MISTER, YOU'RE IN LUCK
NO CRUDE BACK SEAT SUGGESTIONS
SWITCHBLADE IN HER BOOT

the crows talk to her,
give grandmotherly advice
when she needs it most

forgive me, father
for I have sinned, a lot, and
it was pretty great

wedding rings slip off
and disappear till closing
at the broken spoke

old junkies don't feel
broken hearts the same as you
bad love receptors

the roadhouse swayze
in your heart knows that you are
unfuckwithable

the masters tell us
to only write of nature's
beauty. fuck those guys.

they are always there,
learn to be still and listen
to what the dead say

phone calls at midnight
raspy invitations from
the real dirty blonde

you can't begrudge me
for doing the devil's work
that's why you called me

she tried everything
words, god, drugs, love's sweet folly,
swallowing her blues

in the company
of monsters is where I thrive,
the foul-mouthed beauty

NOT iT TASTES
OF DEATH
DIPPED iN M

LIKE METAL
MORE LIKE A SPOON
FOR OIL

I leave a trail of
dirty shirts, coffee cups and
do not disturb signs

you dumped out your purse,
dozens of hotel room keys
hearts you have broken

we've got matching sneers
and matching scarred knuckles, on
fingers intertwined

buy weapons-grade coke,
challenge strangers to duels,
wreak havoc daily.

black and white horror
and cigarette-flavored lips,
a new love to steal

I feign interest
in far too many things just
to appear human

she knows the difference
between good and bad, but makes
exceptions for you

guys like you and me
are living life number nine
dealing atonement

I.

I GOT THE STINK EYE
FROM THE MAID AS SHE WIPED OUR
HANDPRINTS FROM THE WALL

II.

PRAY YOUR ROSARY
MY DEAR, BUT I KNOW WHY YOU
RECOGNIZE MY SIN

YOU CAN'T TAKE A THING
FROM HER, WITH YOUR FORCEFUL HANDS
AND GASOLINE BREATH

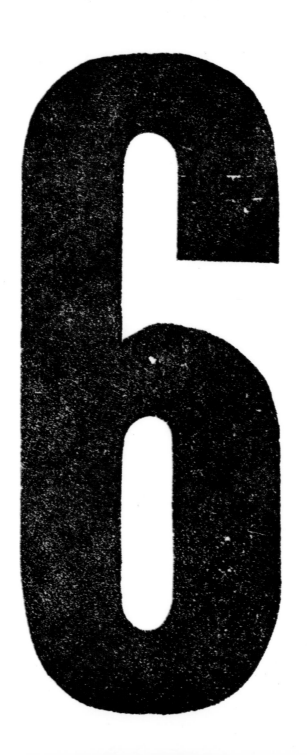

■■■■■■■■■■■■■■■■■■■■■■■■■■■■■■■■■■■■

when the morning comes
you're a howlin' wolf single
scratched up and filthy

at the thunderbird,
where midwestern tourists and
angels fear to tread

I have thirteen days
one for every liquor store
cashier on the ground

when the earth shakes from
god's wrath, I will teach you to
two-step in the ash

***she sang of george and
gracie and cigarette smoke
angels so sweetly***

she is half monster,
throwing bent tiaras out
hotel room windows

the moon is handsome
open your curtains, darlin'
wherever you are

"Brujita!" they yelled.
she thought it sounded pretty,
allowed them to live

listen to freebird
and understand your issues
with intimacy

where do your blues go?
on the pages that you write
or your pillowcase?

my alcoholic
is a werewolf, my full moon
every single night

growing up, we all
fistfight our father's legend.
death wagers on us

the sons of darkness
are seen by no one, my dear
I smile, pearly-white

photos torn in half
not a tear is shed as she
recycles the groom

the days count. every
single one of them. sloth is
the only real sin.

I'm loved and lucky
far beyond all reason, but
mostly I am missed

after each tour
you fight the sickness of still,
pine for the bedlam

he hung bruised and damned
smiling to himself knowing
it was all worth it

one fine day, my dear
I'll add you to my broken
people collection

some nights, she is real,
sleeping next to the altar
other nights, a dream

I paged my sponsor,
I paged my dealer, then I
waited; heads or tails.

when a sentence starts
"a prostitute taught me this"
heads turn in public

I knew you'd be here
vintage slip and cigarettes
suitcase packed, waiting

I HAVE SYLLABLES COHESIVE

SEVENTEEN
TO CONVEY A
THOUGHT, FUCK

you are prone to poor
choices, dear, and I am pleased
to be among them

I.
she's just here to play;
free of the bones and body
that had betrayed her

II.
to wrap around you
and hope you understand; she
couldn't love you more

the second verse of
"you are my sunshine" is a
goddamn wrist-slitter

scratches and bruises
don't linger, the way you kissed
them all better does

under your mattress
your true loves lived, you kissed the
page, staples and all

no smoke and mirrors
or lipstick can disguise that
fucked-up heart of yours

you should know by now
all hearts, even yours, have an
expiration date

all the scarlet mouths,
earthquake hips, and rivers of
jet black hair blind you

you light a camel
I'm jealous of everything
that touches your lips

backwards slow-motion
tongues on repeat, fingernails
digging into hips

something like english,
something familiar, swollen
tongues tell tales of love

when the wheels fall off
this planet, let's turn to ash
in each other's arms

all I remember
is you were here, the rest is
inconsequential

I say kidnapping
is really the most sincere
form of flattery

up close, you whisper
lascivious suggestions,
scribble notes in skin

scorched cities smolder,
the monsters lay dead, she is
innocent, like new

pages soaked in blood,
it was never her nature
to settle for muse

I like my women
just like I like my coffee;
tattooed and slutty

come over, monster
we'll walk around in public
like real people do

spit your incisors
in the sink, your brand new crowns
too sweet to swallow

my prayer candle kiss
and a mattress on the floor
they can't hurt you now

bloody red bouquets
appeared in syringe chambers
then I felt nothing

his ghost in a dream
you check under your pillow
your friend; locked, loaded.

pill organizer
contains antipsychotics
twice daily, with food

your open ribcage,
wanton mouth, your trembling
jesus fucking christ

and the desert waits
for new sin to be added
to its repertoire

we burnt down buildings
that dared to assume they could
ever house a god

the room exploded
she stood amongst her dresses
lips licked, claws sharpened

make peace with your past
that way it's less likely to
fuck up your today

hetropaternal
superfecundation
one hell of a night

what-the-fuck-ever
your nasty little heart wants;
delivered, always

it's true, there is no
I in team but there is a
you in fuck you, man.

you stroll arm in arm,
content with the wolf, knowing
no one can hurt you

feathers fall slowly
as Prince Siegfried and Odette
ascend to heaven

• •

darlin', I hope your
plane doesn't crash, he said. I'm
not done with you yet.

the rain was brutal
I kissed you to shut you up
it still doesn't work

when salty fuck yous
come on valentine's day, they're
best left unanswered

I often lament
"the one who got away" and
why I untied her.

to what's left of you,
from what's left of me: I would
do it all again

• • •

to collapse, crumble
into sheets, given chance to
dream of wine-soaked lips*

DANNY BLAND

once a year he still
romanticizes bushmills
and fair-skinned lasses

GREG DULLI

dark prince, bon vivant
or is he just a mistake
you haven't made, yet

EXENE CERVENKA is the lead vocalist and cofounder of the band X.
She's also a poet and visual artist. Rising to prominence in
the Los Angeles punk rock scene of the late '70s, she continues to
perform with X. Exene has released several books and solo recordings
and currently resides somewhere in the United States.

VICTOR KRUMMENACHER is a musician and art director located in San
Francisco. He's played in a lot of bands, written a lot of songs,
released a bunch of records and designed a lot of stuff, including
this book. He's also a cofounding member of Camper Van Beethoven. He
tries to use his powers for good, but sometimes evil wins.